MY FATHER'S FAITH
BY GRAY HARWELL

INTRODUCTION

Many of you are probably Michiganders, or maybe just baseball lovers. You're familiar with Ernie Harwell, Hall of Fame baseball broadcaster, and voice of the Detroit tigers for 42 years. A large percentage of you might feel like you knew Ernie personally. For many of you he became like a friend as you listened to his warm lyrical play by play night after night, summer after summer. To some in Detroit he became as familiar and essential as Opening Day at Tiger Stadium in April, The Lions game on Thanksgiving, summer trips to your cottage up North, or a Buddy's pizza.

Many of you met Ernie at Tiger Stadium or Comerica Park, or at a book signing, banquet, or Blue Cross Walk in Livonia, Grand Rapids or Traverse City. Some of you got to know Ernie and "Miss Lulu", and had dinner or butter pecan ice cream with them in their home. Some of you are baseball or media professionals who worked with Ernie and knew him as a colleague and friend. When you started in your career he welcomed you and made you feel comfortable in the dugout, in the radio booth or press box. When you were discouraged or struggling, he encouraged and supported you. You knew he was your friend.

Some of you are Tiger fans whose birthdays, anniversaries or illnesses were mentioned by Ernie on his Tiger broadcasts, or with a personal note or phone call. Some of you were in hospitals or retirement homes when he showed up with an autographed baseball in response to your family or friend's request. Some of you were aspiring broadcasters or writers he helped with audition tapes or articles you were putting together.

Most of you knew or sensed that he cared about you as a person. This was true whether you knew him well or had just met him once at the ballpark. This was true if you were an usher or vendor at Tiger Stadium or Al Kaline. There was something different about him. What you probably remembered most about him is that he seemed to genuinely care about you.

From my very personal perspective as Ernie Harwell's youngest son, I want to try to answer three questions that I imagine you might like to ask about my dad.

1. What made Ernie Harwell the man he was?

2. Why did it seem that he really cared about everyone he met?

3. Why was he so universally loved by so many men and women from all walks of life?

I hope you enjoy reading My Father's Faith. I hope it gives you more insight into what made him the man he was.

DEDICATION

To my wonderful wife, Sandy, the love of my life, and our four children, Jeremy, Anne, Joshua, and Elisabeth, who have become amazing people, we're very thankful for.

CONTENTS

"The Giants win the Pennant! The Giants win the Pennant! The Giants win the Pennant!" yelled announcer, Russ Hodges, as the Polo Grounds went crazy with jumping, shouting, New York Giants fans. Bobby Thompson's historic ninth inning home run climaxed the Giant's miraculous comeback to defeat their arch rivals, the Brooklyn Dodgers, and win the 1951 National League Pennant. Hodges' call on the Giants radio broadcast became the most famous sound bite in baseball history, the, "Shot Heard 'Round the World".

Ernie Harwell, the other Giants announcer, was there at the Polo Grounds calling the game for NBC TV, coast to coast. It was the first nationwide sports broadcast on television. Ernie's call was a simple, "It's gone.", as he purposely let the live pictures and sounds of wild celebration on the field and in the stands tell the story.

A Dodger fan listening to Hodges broadcast recorded it and sold it to Hodges for $10. Chesterfield cigarettes, the Giants sponsor, began using the recording and it soon became baseball history.

Ernie Harwell's historic telecast of one of baseball's most memorable moments wasn't recorded and therefore has never been heard, except by those who heard it live on October 3, 1951. "It's gone." became an apt description both for Thompson's home run and Harwell's broadcast.

LEARNING TO LOVE THE GAME

Ernie Harwell had loved baseball since his boyhood in Atlanta, Georgia in the 20's. His dad, Gray, taught him to love the scratchy sound of the game coming through a crystal set. He remembered hearing Graham McNamee's broadcast of the 1926 World Series when the Cardinals beat the Yankees by throwing out Babe Ruth, who was trying to steal second in the ninth inning of game seven. He listened intently when his dad talked about his friend, Sherrod Smith, who had pitched for the Brooklyn Dodgers against Ruth and the Yankees in 1916 World Series.

He had fond memories of going to Atlanta Crackers games at Ponce de Leon Park with his dad and seeing his first major league game at Comiskey Park in Chicago in 1934 with his great uncle, Lauren Foreman.

As a boy, Ernie loved playing baseball even more than he did watching it in person or hearing it on radio. He started playing sandlot ball with other boys from his neighborhood and by age 11 worked his way up to the Piedmont Pirates All Star Team. His next step was American Legion Baseball with the North Side Terrors. They made it to the championship game at Ponce de Leon Park against the Grant Park Aces. Although he was spunky and enthusiastic, Ernie admitted he didn't hit well enough or run fast enough to make it any farther as a player. His love for baseball would have to find another outlet.

IN THE GAME

At the ripe old age of 16, Ernie wrote a letter to his favorite baseball newspaper, The Sporting News, under the name "W. Ernest Harwell". His purpose was to persuade them that they needed an Atlanta correspondent, and it should be him. Not realizing he was only 16 and had never written anything before, they hired him. This unlikely beginning with the Sporting News eventually led to a long relationship with the paper and its editor, an historic character in baseball, J.G. Taylor Spink. Ernie's surprising opportunity with The Sporting News was only the beginning of seventy five years experiencing baseball history.

Ernie Harwell's love and passion for baseball would be rewarded with extraordinary opportunities to become friends with many of its most important players, managers, owners and announcers, while broadcasting some of baseball's greatest moments.

In 1940 Ernie graduated from Emory University and became the first Sports Director of WSB in Atlanta. Even as a newcomer in radio he had the chance to interview icons who played a major role in baseball. The legendary Connie Mack, who played and managed for 61 years in the major leagues, was one of Ernie's early guests on WSB. Babe Ruth was another.

Twenty four year old Red Sox slugger, Ted Williams, visited WSB's makeshift studio in a hotel room at the Atlanta Biltmore to talk with Ernie on air. Harwell even left the studio to attempt a rare interview with the infamous Ty Cobb at his home in Royston, Georgia. Cobb was known for his rough behavior on and off the field and was not usually welcoming to reporters, especially after his retirement. He surprised everyone by talking cordially with Ernie on tape for his WSB show. Even more surprising, Cobb and Ernie developed an ongoing friendship that lasted many years.

PLAY BY PLAY

The young broadcaster's next chance to rub shoulders with baseball history happened because he was hired to do play by play with his favorite team, the Atlanta Crackers, in 1943. Ernie's stint with the Marines in WWII interrupted his new job until after the war. In 1948 Brooklyn President, Branch Rickey, told Ernie's boss, Earl Mann, that he wanted Ernie to fill in for ailing Red Barber on the Dodgers radio broadcast. Mann agreed to trade Ernie for Minor league catcher, Cliff Dapper, and Harwell became the first and only announcer traded for a player.

This minor event led to a much more significant opportunity for Ernie to experience first hand what he considered the most important event in baseball and sports history. Branch Rickey had signed the incredibly talented Jackie Robinson to play for the Dodgers a year before in 1947. It was the beginning of the end for racial segregation in baseball, but change never comes easy.

Ernie was a Southerner, a Georgian, whose boyhood love for baseball was incubated watching his heroes, the Atlanta Crackers play at Ponce de Leon Park. Being a play by play announcer for the Crackers for three years deepened his connection with everything about baseball in Atlanta and the South. Ernie was with the Dodgers when they arrived in Atlanta in the spring of 1949 to play three exhibition games against the Crackers. Vestiges of the Ku Klux Klan were still trying to intimidate and influence Georgians. They saw Jackie Robinson's appearance in Atlanta with the Dodgers as a chance to turn back the clock.

The Klan let Earl Mann and the Crackers know that if Jackie Robinson played at Ponce de Leon Park, he would be assassinated. Jackie wouldn't be intimidated and neither would the Crackers or Dodgers. One of the Dodgers jokingly suggested that they should all wear Jackie's Number on their backs and see what happened. Nothing did happen. Jackie played in all three games without any trouble. Ernie was pleased to witness a first in his hometown – blacks and whites competing together in a professional sports event.

Jackie Robinson and Ernie Harwell and their wives, Rachel and Lula, became good friends in '48 and '49. Ernie enjoyed playing cards on the train with Jackie and the other "Boys of Summer', Pee Wee Reese, Gil Hodges, Billy Cox, Carl Furillo, Roy Campanella, etc. Lula, Rachel, and other Dodger's wives would often have dinner together in the city when their husbands were on the road.

In his second year in the Dodgers' booth with Red Barber and Connie Desmond, Ernie watched Jackie Robinson lead his team into the World Series while winning the NL batting title and MVP. It wasn't Jackie's speed on the bases or even his great ability as a hitter that impressed Ernie most

> To me the most impressive thing about Jackie was his combative attitude, the way he always wanted to win. He was very aggressive and he didn't let anything stand in his way. I think that made him an ideal choice to break the color line. Rickey had to pick a player that was good, near great, and he had to get a guy who was aggressive and who had the qualities of leadership. Jackie answered him in all those phases.[1]

Looking back on his exciting years of watching and broadcasting Jackie Robinson's historic success, Ernie believes he witnessed the most significant change that ever happened in baseball and the world of sports. He believed that Branch Rickey and Jackie Robinson's successful "experiment' opened the way for all of the talented athletes from many races and cultures to excel in baseball and all the other sports.

ERNIE AND THE GIANTS

Ernie moved across town in 1950 to join the New York Giants and partner with Russ Hodges in their radio broadcasts. He was just in time to experience the debut of one of baseball's greatest players and to call one of the game's most memorable seasons.

In May of 1951 the Giants welcomed their best prospect, 20 year old Willie Mays, from their Minneapolis farm team. The Giants, their fans and the media were excited to see what the young centerfielder, who was batting .477 in the minors, could do in the big leagues. Willie went 0 for 12 in his first three games at Philadelphia and before his first start in New York asked his manager, Leo Durocher, to send him back to Minneapolis. Ernie said that Durocher replied, "As long as I'm manager here, you're my centerfielder. I know you can do the job; now go out there tonight and do it."[2]

Willie responded by pounding a home run to left his first time at bat, against Warren Spahn. It turned out to be his only hit in his first 25 at bats, but he soon settled down and went on to become Rookie of The Year in 1951. It was one of Harwell's greatest thrills to broadcast the rookie year of the future Hall of Famer and one of baseball's all time greats. Ernie and Willie became life long friends. Whenever he was asked who was the greatest ball player he had ever seen, Ernie always answered, and without hesitation, "Willie Mays".

Nineteen fifty one was also the one of the most memorable seasons of Major League Baseball because of the intense rivalry between The Brooklyn Dodgers and The New York Giants for the National League Pennant. Because of his two years with Brooklyn before coming to the Giants, Ernie Harwell understood the heated competition between these two teams and their fans, and thoroughly enjoyed the excitement it generated in New York and beyond. The Polo Grounds and Ebbets Field were only a few miles apart and the winning team would stay in the city to play the American League Champion, New York Yankees, in the World Series. To add to the drama, the Giants won 37 of their last 44 games to catch the Dodgers from 13 ½ games behind in August, and force a three game playoff with the Dodgers for the Pennant.

All of this suspense led to Bobby Thompson's home run, The "Shot Heard 'Round the World", which gave the Giants the NL Pennant in one of the most dramatic victories in baseball history.

During Ernie Harwell's five years in New York with the Dodgers and Giants he became close friends with legendary players Jackie Robinson, Duke Snyder, Gil Hodges, Roy Campenella, Pee Wee Reese, Willie Mays, Bobby Thompson, Monte Irvin, Eddie Stanky, Alvin Dark and others. He covered Jackie Robinsons' early success and witnessed his historic impact on racial discrimination in sports. He also broadcast the debut and development of one of the greatest players of all time, Willie Mays, while doing play by play of the classic battle between the Giants and Dodgers in 1951.

THE ORIOLES AND ERNIE ENTER THE AMERICAN LEAGUE

Ernie left New York for the exciting opportunity to be the first announcer of the Baltimore Orioles, as they entered the American League in 1954. It was stimulating to the baseball historian in Harwell to cover the beginnings of a new team in Baltimore which already had a long history as The St. Louis Browns. The Orioles also had a long tradition in Baltimore which included Jack Dunn's discovery of Babe Ruth and Lefty Grove in the early 1900's. Baseball legends Connie Mack, Hank Greenberg, and Lefty Grove were some of those who officially welcomed the Orioles into the American League at their first game.

Unfortunately for Harwell, the Orioles were a typical new team. They lost 100 games their first year and continued to struggle through Ernie's six years in Baltimore.

Highlights for him were watching young rookie, Brooks Robinson, develop into a Hall of Fame third baseman, working with two future Hall of Fame broadcasters, Herb Carneal and Chuck Thompson, and getting to know one of most quirky and knowledgeable men in the game, Orioles Manager, Paul Richards.

Although the Orioles performance on the field was dismal, Ernie enjoyed many of the players, managers and executives who became his friends in Baltimore. During his years with the Orioles he also wrote his personal definition of baseball, "A Game for All America", which hangs in The Baseball Hall of Fame.

TIGER HISTORY

Ernie Harwell's next forty two years watching and calling baseball history would take place with one of the game's greatest teams, The Detroit Tigers. In 1960 the Tigers asked Ernie to join his old friend, George Kell, in the tiny green WJR broadcast booth that hung from the upper deck of Briggs Stadium. Harwell was grateful for the opportunity to be part of one of baseball's most storied franchises whose history included legends Ty Cobb, Harry Heilmann, Hank Greenberg, Charlie Gehringer, Harvey Kuenn, Hal Newhouser, and Dizzy Trout. Major league baseball had been played at the corner of Michigan and Trumbull since 1901 and Detroiters were known for their undying loyalty and passion for their home team.

The solid Tigers of the early 60's became pennant contenders in 1967 when four American League teams were fighting for the title on the last day of the season. The Red Sox beat out the White Sox, Minnesota and the Tigers, who lost by splitting back to back double headers. 1967 had been a traumatic year of violent riots in Detroit and the Tigers had hoped to boost the city's spirits with a trip to the World Series that fall.

1968 was going to be the year that the Tigers brought healing to a scarred and divided city. The victory that the team, the city, and Ernie Harwell had hoped for in '67 would become reality in '68.

Denny McClain would win 31 games, the Cy Young and the MVP with a 1.96 ERA. Jim Northrup would have 90 RBIs, Willie Horton 36 homers, phenomenal pinch hitter, Gates Brown, would hit .370, but these great individual performances weren't really the story. The team spirit of players who had played together for years and their devastating last day loss in '67 brought them to Spring Training with a passion and confidence to win. They did win 103 games, leading the league in runs and homers and beating second place Baltimore, by 12 games.

It was a thrill for Ernie Harwell to be there to call the Tiger's first pennant winning season in 23 years. He was looking forward to broadcasting a classic World Series against the Cardinals and their MVP and Cy Young winner, Bob Gibson.

Gibson beat McClain in the first game 4-0. Mickey Lolich bested the Cards 8-1 in game two. Almost everything went wrong for the Tigers in games three and four with Gibson beating McClain again, 10-1, in game four. Detroit was faced with having to win games five, six, and seven against the confident Cardinals. Lolich pitched courageously to win game five, 5-3. In game six McClain won his only game of the series 13-1, with the help of Jim Northup's grand slam and a record tying ten run third inning.

Ernie was broadcasting the World Series classic he'd always dreamed of - a game seven duel between future Hall of Famer, Bob Gibson, and his reigning World Champion Cardinals vs. the surprising Mickey Lolich and the "comeback" Tigers. It was a tense, scoreless battle into the seventh when Northrup came to bat with two out and Cash and Horton on the bases. "Now the set by Gibson. We're ready. There's a swing and a fly ball to center – here comes Flood digging hard. He almost fell down. It's over his head for a hit – Cash is rounding third – he scores. Willie Horton rounds third – he scores. Northrup goes on to third base, Detroit leads, 2-0."[3], said the excited Harwell. Lolich stayed tough through the final two innings, holding St. Louis to only one run on five hits. He out pitched Gibson 4-1, winning his third game of the series and giving the Tigers their first World Championship since 1945.

CHARACTERS OF THE 70'S

After their dramatic World Series win in '68, the Tigers reached the post season only once in the next 15 years, losing to Oakland for the AL Championship in '72. What characterized the Tigers in the 70's were its characters – Billy Martin, Ron Leflore and Mark "The Bird" Fidrych.

Ernie Harwell saw a parade of seven managers come and go in the 70's. The biggest character of them all was Billy Martin. When he came to manage the Tigers in 1971 he turned them around, bringing them into a second place finish in their division. In '72 they won the Eastern Division but lost to Oakland in game 5 of the League Championship. By the end of the season in '73 Billy was fired. Ernie said

> It was the same pattern that followed Martin wherever he went – Minnesota, Detroit, Texas, New York, and Oakland. Billy is always off to a good start, hailed as the hero by the man- in- the-street, and then somehow attrition sets in. He rubs someone in the front office the wrong way, strife ensues, and Billy Martin walks again.... All in all, Billy was self-destructive. While he was in Detroit the going cliché was "Billy Martin's biggest problem is Billy Martin."[4]

Billy Martin, Ernie Harwell, Lou Matlin, Frank Howard and Jimmy Butsacaris were an odd group on an unusual assignment to Jackson Prison in May, 1973. Matlin, Director of Community Affairs for the Tigers, wanted some of the players to talk with the inmates and Jimmy Butsacaris wanted Billy Martin to meet an inmate named Ron Leflore, who'd been writing Butsacaris. When Billy Martin met Leflore in the prison hospital that day he told Billy, "I'd like a chance with the Tigers." Billy agreed to give him a tryout when Ron was ready for parole. A few months later Martin kept his word, and gave Leflore two chances to show him what he could do. Ernie was at the first tryout at Tiger Stadium. "I saw him hit several drives in the stands. I saw his great running speed and his raw ability."[6] Billy Martin saw it too and was convinced Ron Leflore could be an asset to the team. Detroit signed Leflore in July.

By the end of next season Leflore was on the Tiger roster and Billy Martin was gone. Ron's exceptional natural abilities gave him five good years at Detroit. In '78 he led the American League in stolen bases and runs scored. A Detroit sports writer told his story of transformation from prisoner to major league star. It became a movie.

Sadly, there wasn't a happy ending as Leflore reverted to some of his former weaknesses, didn't get along with managers, Sparky Anderson, or White Sox manager, Tony LaRussa, and ended up getting busted for drugs in '82. Ernie Harwell told us, "I had a special feeling for Ron. I was there when he was discovered. He was warm and friendly to me. He had visited my home and eaten dinner with my family. My heart ached when he blew his chance to become a very special kind of baseball hero."[7]

The third and most popular and colorful of the characters that appeared in the Detroit uniform in the 70's was Mark "The Bird" Fidrych. Although he'd been part of the Tiger organization for three years, no one paid him much attention until Spring Training in 1976. Manager, Ralph Houk, put him on the team but didn't start him until mid May.

He amazed everyone by winning 19 games and becoming a super star that baseball fans in every town wanted to see. Whenever he pitched he would draw crowds who enjoyed his crazy antics on the field. His height and thin build coupled with his angular jerky movements made him look like Big Bird on Sesame Street. He was animated and enthusiastic, talking to the baseball, shaking hands with his infielders, and jumping in the air when his team made a play. Ernie enjoyed recounting the crazy way he expressed himself.

> Early in that first year Houk had to move the Bird to the far end of the dugout to avoid ear drum damage from Mark's constant cheerleading. Once during a rally, Fidrych shouted, "Come on gang. Remember a hit is as good as a walk". Later when Mickey Stanley was thrown out attempting to steal third base, Fidrych yelled, "All right, team, let's capitalize on that now." He frequently took curtain calls after a victory, reveling in the moment and the applause of the crowd.[8]

Unfortunately, the magic didn't last. Mark injured his knee in Spring Training in 1977, then started having arm problems. He was never able to pitch effectively again.

But for one extraordinary season in the somewhat lackluster 70's, Mark "The Bird" Fidrych brought excitement and huge ticket sales to Detroit and their American League rivals.

"THE BLESS YOU BOYS" OF '84

Detroit regained their competitive edge in the 80's under the capable management of Sparky Anderson. They finished two games back in '81, and were second in '83. Like the '68 team, they came to Spring Training in '84 with confidence and a strong desire to win. The team was also loaded with talent. They had the great double play combination of Trammell and Whitaker; the best starter in the league, Jack Morris; Willie Hernandez, who would win the Cy Young and MVP for his effectiveness in relief; Kirk Gibson and Lance Parrish, who could supply the power; and veteran, Darrell Evans, who could help keep the younger players focused and steady.

Their record speaks for itself. Jack Morris pitched an early no hitter on April 7, the motivated Tigers won their first nine games, and then set a major league record winning 35 of their first 40 games. They finished 104-58, 15 games ahead of Toronto and then swept Kansas City in the American League Championship

Detroit was ecstatic about their "Bless You Boys". They broke attendance records at Tiger Stadium, selling 2,704,794 tickets. It had been an historic year for the Tigers and their fans, reminiscent of the glories of '68. Eighty-four was one of Ernie Harwell's favorite seasons, of the fifty-five he broadcast in the major leagues. The team had great chemistry and a sense of unity and destiny about it. It wasn't so much about the individual players, their egos and accomplishments, as it was about the team. It seemed that a different player almost every game would make the play or get the hit which give the team victory. Often a utility player or someone off the bench made the winning contribution. One moment that epitomized the '84 Tigers for Ernie Harwell was Dave Bergman batting with two on base and two out in the tenth inning of a tie game against Toronto. The outcome was important psychologically because the Blue Jays were the Tigers closest rival and this was the first game of their first series in '84. With two strikes against him, Bergman fought off seven pitches and then slammed the eighth into the right-field stands for a 6-3 Tiger victory.

Sparky Anderson, and Bergman's teammates, as Ernie described it, "were amazed at both the intensity and concentration Bergman showed in his one-on-one battle with Blue Jays pitcher, Roy Lee Jackson. To me it was a symbol of the season. Bergman was not a superstar. He was a player who came along as extra baggage in the Willie Hernandez deal. He was a hard-nosed, dedicated professional. He was a role player. He did not play every day but was always ready when his manager needed him."[9] Later in the season, "He was facing Toronto again- this time in Toronto. He banged out four hits against Blue Jay pitching. His final hit was another three –run home run- again in the tenth inning- which gave the Tigers a 7-4 win. That victory put the Detroiters 9 ½ games ahead of the Jays and settled the Eastern Division race."[10]

Winning 104 games and sweeping KC in the AL Championship gave Detroit a lot of confidence and momentum going into the World Series of '84.

Jack Morris won the first game of the series in San Diego 3-2. He shut out the Padres for eight innings after allowing two runs in the first. San Diego came back in game two, 5-3. Back in Detroit, the home team won game three, 5-2, on the excellent pitching of Milt Wilcox and Willie Hernandez. The Tigers showed their dominating pitching and their power in games four and five. In game four Morris went all the way giving up only 2 runs on five hits. Alan Trammell drove in all 4 Detroit runs, hitting two homers with a man on base. Kirk Gibson's 2 homers and 5 RBIs lead the Tigers to an exciting 8-4 victory in game 5. It was Gibby's eighth inning blast that sealed the championship for Detroit. Here's Ernie's famous call. "Ball one on Kirk. Here's the pitch. He swings, there's a long drive to right! And it's a home run for Gibson! A three run homer! The Tigers lead it, 8-4, in the eighth inning!"[11]

Detroit had won its second World Series Championship in 16 years as they eliminated San Diego in just five games. Alan Trammell was MVP with a .450 average, 2 homers, and 6 RBIs. Kirk Gibson batted .333 and contributed 2 homers and 7 RBIs. Jack Morris won 2 games with a 2.00 ERA, and Willie Hernandez pitched 5 innings in relief with a 1.69 ERA. Detroit won the Eastern Division, the American League, and the World Championship all at home in Tiger Stadium in 1984!

Although Ernie Harwell thoroughly enjoyed broadcasting a second historic World Series Victory for the Tigers in 1984, his long time broadcasting partner, Paul Carey and his wife, Patti, were heavy on his mind.

To me, the greatest performance of the World Series didn't happen on the diamond. It happened in our radio booth. It was the performance of Paul Carey who worked under tension and pressure that would have been unbearable for a lesser man.

He broadcast most of the series knowing that his wife, Patty, had been stricken with a malignant brain tumor.

Still, there was a job to be done. And he did it. It was his first World Series broadcast—something he'd dreamed of since boyhood. The team he had loved since his Mt. Pleasant boyhood was competing in the World Series with him at the microphone.

Here he was in the midst of the happiest time for the Tigers. They had swept the season and the playoffs and now they were winning the World Series.

But for Paul, it was the saddest time of his life.

Finally the Tigers won. Paul went to the clubhouse. His heart was heavy, but he became a part of the jubilation of the championship clubhouse. Wet with champagne, he shouted congratulations to the players and elicited their happy yells and comments.

So to me the best, the gutsiest performance of the 1984 World Series was that of my partner Paul Carey.[12]

After their amazing season in 1984, the Tigers made it to the post season only once during the rest of Ernie Harwell's years with Detroit. They lost to Minnesota, 4-1, in the '87 American League Championship.

OFF WITH THE OLD, ON WITH THE NEW

The most significant and historical events in Detroit baseball in the 90's were the end of eighty eight years of Major League play at the corner of Michigan and Trumbull and changes in the ownership of the Tigers. Many Detroit fans, including Ernie Harwell, had tried to find a way to save aging Tiger Stadium. All efforts failed and on September 27, 1999 a full house watched the Tigers win their last game at the historic "Corner". Over 60 former Tigers, including most of the stars of the '68 and '84 World Champions, appeared on the field after the game. Ernie was given the honor of saying the final good bye.

Tonight we say good-bye. But we will not forget. Open your eyes, look around and take a mental picture. Moments like this shall live on forever.

It's been 88 moving years at Michigan and Trumbull. The tradition built here shall endure along with the permanence of the Olde English D. But tonight we must say good-bye.

Farewell old friend, Tiger Stadium. We will remember."

A new century of Tiger history began on April 11, 2000, with the first game at Comerica Park, only about a mile northeast of old Tiger Stadium. A sold out crowd braved a 34 degree chill to watch the home team defeat Seattle, 5-2. The new Tiger home included a "Walk of Fame", statues, famous names on the outfield walls, and many other tributes to Tiger history. Ernie Harwell wasn't forgotten. Over the main gate stood a huge metallic black and white picture of him at his mic calling some "looong gone" moment in tiger history. His statue is also here just inside the gate and his name on the center field wall next to Cochrane and Kell.

After the end of the 2002 season Ernie Harwell said his farewell to the Tigers and his many fans.

The Tigers have just finished their 2002 season, and I have finished my baseball broadcasting career. It's time to say goodbye, but goodbyes are sad, so I'd rather say hello. Hello to a new adventure. I'm not leaving. I'll still be here with you, living my life in Michigan, surrounded by family and friends. Rather than say goodbye, please allow me to say thank you. Thank you for letting me be apart of your family. Thank you for taking me with you to the cottage up north, to the beach, the picnic, your workplace and the backyard. Thank you for sneaking your transistor under the pillow as you grew up loving the Tigers. I might have been a small part of your life, but you have been a large part of mine. It was my privilege and honor to share with you the greatest game of all. Now God has a new adventure for me and I'm ready to move on. So I leave you with a deep sense of appreciation for your longtime loyalty and support. Thank you very much and God bless you.

CHAPTER TWO - CONTENTMENT AND CRISIS

After my dad, Ernie Harwell, retired from the Tigers at eighty-four, he was still as active as ever. His main endeavor was being the spokesperson for Michigan Blue Cross/Blue Shield. He loved traveling around Michigan, leading "walks" and speaking at luncheons and dinners in Detroit, Grand Rapids, Traverse City, and other cities all over the state. He was perfect for the job because he loved people and had always kept himself fit with a healthy diet, and a daily regimen of exercise. He really enjoyed encouraging people to keep healthy and active. He also loved talking Tiger baseball with Michiganders, wherever the Blues sent him.

Dad also kept busy writing a weekly column for the Free Press, recording "Ernie Harwell's Audio Scrapbook", doing endorsements and commercials, speaking to churches and other groups and enjoying time with the family. During the Tigers' postseason appearance in 2006, dad even got back in the broadcast booth with ESPN TV and the Tigers' radio network.

In his late eighties, dad was sharper, both mentally and physically, than most men in their 50's. He always got up early in the morning to spend time reading his Bible and praying before breakfast. He would give at least an hour almost every day to working out in the gym. He loved to keep mentally fit with crossword puzzles and reading. He could quote baseball stats from the 20's, 60's or 80's like he'd just read them in the paper. I'd sometimes overhear him doing a radio interview and reeling off batting averages and ERAs long forgotten by everyone, except him. Mom, being a normal woman in her eighties, would often have trouble remembering the names of their many neighbors at Fox Run. Not dad. He knew the names of all of the "inmates", as he jokingly called them, and would whisper their names to mom whenever she drew a blank. He was amazing. Whenever anyone asked me how dad was doing I'd have to confess that even though he was 28 years older than his son, he could still run circles around me.

Dad and mom really enjoyed their time together after his "retirement" in 2002. With dad broadcasting major league baseball for 55 of their 60+ years of marriage, they hadn't had a lot of time together during all those long baseball seasons. Mom relished just having dad around and being able to spend time with him. They enjoyed going together on weekend trips around the state, being with family in Michigan, visiting with me and my family and other relatives and friends in Atlanta, and spending part of their winters in Florida. Dad had adjusted very well to the slower pace of being at home with mom most of the time. He seemed very relaxed and content not to be traveling and receiving the constant stimulation and admiration he had enjoyed for so many years. Dad and mom had a sweet seven year season of enjoying each other more than they ever had before. Then suddenly the unexpected news came that shattered their contentment.

THE CALL I THOUGHT I'D NEVER RECEIVE

In August, 2009, I got the phone call I thought I'd never receive. It was my dad. He was calmly telling me that he'd just gotten news of his recent tests at Ford Hospital. He said, rather matter of factly, "The tests show that I have bile duct cancer. The doctors are giving me about six months to live". Amazingly, he went on to assure me that he was trusting God and looking forward to his "new adventure" in Heaven. Steadying myself, I tried to reinforce his confidence in God, prayed with him, and told him I loved him.

I was shocked, dumbfounded. It couldn't be. My dad, the "poster boy", of senior health and vitality, who seemed forever young and full of life, was dying.

Just a few weeks before, our whole family had enjoyed a great celebration of my mother's ninetieth birthday. Dad had been so typically enthusiastic and supportive of our plans for all the children, grandchildren, and great grandchildren to surprise her on her birthday. We'd flown in from New York, Boston, Atlanta and Florida. We all had a wonderful time laughing over old family stories, celebrating with mom, and having dad give us his own personal tour of Comerica Park.

He happily led an entourage of "Miss Lulu", my wife, Sandy, and me, our four adult children, two of their spouses, three great grandchildren, and my sister into the Tiger's locker room and dugout, onto the field, out to his statue, and upstairs to the new Ernie Harwell Media Center.

While we were there for mom's ninetieth birthday, dad told Sandy and me that he was having some minor digestive problems, which he thought were related to what he called "his gerd". None of us knew or even imagined he had any serious health issues. We all knew that he was very disciplined about his daily workouts and diet and received regular and extensive check ups with his doctors.

At ninety-one he still had four years on his contract as spokesman for Michigan Blue Cross / Blue Shield, which could be renewed at ninety–five for another ten years. It always seemed to us that dad would never lose his health or "joie de vivre", and that he'd probably outlive us all. There was also a prevailing sense that because of his faith and the way he'd lived his life, no serious disease would attack him.

None of us Harwells could imagine our lives without him. He had always been the glue that held us together, the voice of reason, and the one who would help see us through any struggles we faced. He gave us strength and stability. He was always there for us. Dad gave so much to each and all of us and we knew it would never be the same without him.

We all know that diseases and suffering can and do happen to those we're certain don't deserve them. In spite of this, somehow we still don't expect those who have lived like dad to be visited with cancer or calamity.

The reality is that the "good" are not exempt from trouble and pain but that those who know and trust God are able to overcome whatever comes their way through His amazing love and grace.

Dad, even in dying, was actually still more concerned about others than himself. His first thought was Lulu, his faithful wife and best friend for almost seventy years.

He wanted to take care of her, console, and comfort her. He wanted to spend his final days just being with her and helping her accept and overcome their looming separation. Mom's response to the doctors' grim conclusions had understandably been more intense than the rest of the family. She was deeply shocked and saddened with the reality that her beloved Ernie would be leaving her behind. Dad was constantly encouraging her that their separation would be only temporary because they would soon be together again in Heaven.

Dad was also thinking more about his children than himself. He was doing every thing he could to help Bill, Carolyn, Julie and me, accept and prepare for our impending loss. He was giving more of his time talking with us, reassuring us, and just being there for us.

Beyond our family, my father continued to see some of his friends and fans, even still signing baseballs and answering some of his phone calls and mail. So many well wishers and autograph collectors were showing up at the door of his apartment in Novi that we were forced to tape a sign to his door asking people not to disturb dad and mom because they needed to rest.

FAREWELLS

On September 16, about a month after the public announcement of his terminal illness, the Tigers gave a special farewell for dad at Comerica Park, between the third and fourth innings of a night game with the Royals. He gave a short talk to the Tigers in their clubhouse before the game, and was honored with a video presentation of his career in baseball. The Tigers and the Royals stood respectfully on the dugout steps and the whole Comerica crowd rose to their feet as dad walked towards home plate to say his final goodbye.

Raising his arms to acknowledge the overwhelming applause, he quieted the crowd. As always, his words were brief and to the point.

In my almost 92 years on this earth, the good Lord has blessed me with a great journey. And the blessed part of that journey is that it's going to end here in the great state of Michigan. I deeply appreciate the people of Michigan. I love their grit.

I love the way they face life. I love the family values they have. And you Tiger fans are the greatest fans of all. No question about that. I certainly want to thank you from the depth of my heart for your devotion, your support, your loyalty and your love. Thank you very much and God bless you.

Just four days after the Tiger farewell the Lions honored dad at Ford Field during halftime of their home opener against the Minnesota Vikings. Looking very thin in a too large, blue "HARWELL 1", Lions jersey, he said goodbye again, this time to 56,000 wildly applauding Lions Fans. The amazing displays of love and support he received at Comerica Park and Ford Field, as well as all the many letters and cards coming daily from friends and fans all over the country, energized dad.

It was a bittersweet time for a dying man. He was encouraged and comforted by the overwhelming love and appreciation coming from so many whose lives he had touched. He wanted to continue acknowledging and responding to everyone, but his advancing cancer wouldn't allow his body to keep up.

In late September dad was severely weakened by a serious infection. He spent several days in Ford Hospital while his doctors brought the infection under control. His friend, Mitch Albom, had invited him to appear at an evening fund raiser at Detroit's Fox Theatre on September 30th. Dad's doctors didn't want him to compromise his condition by getting out of bed and going out at night to such a public venue. However, his desire to support Mitch's cause and to share his faith with those at the Fox prevailed. Weak and still hot with a one hundred and two fever, he appeared on stage with Mitch Albom, telling him and the sold out crowd that he knew, "into whose arms I'm gonna fall", "where I'm going and what a great, great thing Heaven is going to be".

"GOD REMAINS THE STRENGTH"

The Fall of 2009 was a very difficult time for dad and mom and our whole family. In our heads we knew dad was dying but our hearts weren't welcoming the hard truth of our impending loss. Mom's shock and sorrow could be heard in her voice and seen on her face.

How could she accept the reality of losing her first love, her best friend, her soul mate for almost seventy years?

There were good days and bad. Some days dad would be feeling pretty well physically and would take mom out for lunch at one of their favorite nearby restaurants. On those days they savored their precious, dwindling hours together. They had a bittersweet joy in their hearts which made their painful future seem somehow less imminent and overwhelming.

Still, that Fall our lives were an emotional roller coaster. Dad and mom's treasured times together would suddenly turn into days of difficulty, discomfort, and uncertainty. Dad had several serious infections, numerous tests, and a few procedures related to his cancer which required hospitalization. We wondered each time if he was nearing the end or if this was just another challenge he had to weather. As always, dad would do his best to be positive and encourage mom and the rest of us, in spite of his own discomfort and pain. Several times when he recovered and returned home from the hospital, dad seemed almost like his old self again and his cancer like a bad dream that had faded with the first bright rays of morning light.

Because I was living in Southwest Florida and wasn't able to be with dad and mom during most of this time, I talked with them by phone almost every day.

I tried to encourage both of them with the news and exploits of our children and grandchildren, by reading them verses from Psalms, and by praying for them over the phone. There were some especially poignant times with dad when a verse, or a passage of scripture, or my words in prayer would move him.

I remember back in August when dad first called with the sad news of his cancer. I read to him from Psalm 73.

> Yet I still belong to you;
> you are holding my right hand.
> You will keep on guiding me with your counsel,
> leading me to a glorious destiny.

Whom have I in heaven but you?
I desire you more than anything on earth.
My health may fail, and my spirit may grow weak,
but God remains the strength of my heart;
he is mine forever.-

But as for me, how good it is to be near God!
I have made the Sovereign Lord my shelter,
and I will tell everyone about the wonderful things
you do. (Psalm 73:23-28 NLT).[13]

I sensed that those verses really resonated with him that day. He told me several months later that they were something he held on to, that greatly encouraged him through this tough time.

Sometime around Thanksgiving I suggested to dad that it would be great for him to share the story of his faith on video. He was very responsive to the idea. It would give him an opportunity to tell people about his faith in a more candid and personal way than ever before. We agreed to write the script for the interview together and I asked my youngest son, Josh, if he would help us produce the video. Josh was happy to handle the technical aspects and make it three generations of Harwells working together.

Dad, Josh, and I wrote the interview script together in December. We enjoyed working together over the phone and via the internet, developing the questions and responses that would tell the story of dad's career in baseball, how he'd seen God at work in the Major Leagues, and most importantly, his own personal journey of faith. It seemed good for all of us to do something positive together that we hoped would become part of dad's legacy.

Josh and I scheduled flights to Detroit for January 9, 2010, to shoot the video with dad. He wasn't feeling very well the week before and I suggested to him that we postpone or even cancel our plans for the video, arguing that his health and comfort should take top priority. His ninety-second birthday was just weeks away, maybe we could do it then, if he felt better.

He said he didn't want to wait and he wouldn't hear of not going ahead with our plans to shoot the video on the January 9th.

Josh and I landed in Detroit just after noon on the 9th and went straight to Novi to see dad. When we arrived at his apartment mom met us at the door. She was obviously upset and told us that dad was very weak and nauseated, and that his doctor was on the way. Josh and I were surprised and concerned to see him looking so pale and thin. We talked with him very briefly and prayed for him before his doctor arrived.

A few minutes later he was on his way to Henry Ford Hospital in West Bloomfield. We visited him there later that day and enjoyed a little more relaxed time with him again the next day, before we had to go home. Praying for dad and mom on my flight back to Ft. Myers, I wondered how much longer dad would be with us.

In just a few days he was back in his apartment with mom, feeling much better. We all breathed a sigh of relief and were thankful that our emotional roller coaster was back on the up swing.

A friend of mine who lives in Bloomfield Hills, Michigan, told me he would like to help us produce the video of dad. He could get a professional cameraman to go with him to dad's apartment and shoot the video. I asked dad if he still wanted to do it and how he felt about us adapting our script from an interview to just him, "solo on the sofa". He still wanted to do it and didn't mind going it alone. He had done so many interviews with everyone from local media to Larry King and Bob Costas, but he'd never done a video focused on his faith. He wasn't about to forego this opportunity because of his age, his advancing cancer, or any other circumstance. My friend and our camera and sound man, came to dad's apartment two days after his ninety-second birthday and recorded his story. Dad was amazing. He was so natural, so honest, so candid and down to earth. When you watch the video you almost feel like you're sitting there with him in his living room, waiting for "Miss Lulu" to serve you some ice cream. His sincerity, honesty and humility about his relationship with God were really refreshing and inspirational.

Over the next three months dad continued to have his physical ups and downs, but his cancer was progressing and making him increasingly uncomfortable. His appetite, weight and strength were on a slow but steady decline. He wasn't sleeping soundly or longer than a few hours at a time. Mom was continually at his side trying to keep him comfortable. He wasn't seeing anyone except family, a few of his closest friends, and his doctors. He rarely left his apartment.

LOOKING UP

This was a very tough time for him. In addition to his physical and emotional challenges he was housebound, and without the usual stimulation of his many friends and having something to set his hand to. His whole life dad had thrived on being involved with people, keeping mentally and physically active and being productive. Although this was probably the most difficult and trying time of his life, dad still wouldn't complain or feel sorry for himself.

As much as he could, he tried to focus on "what a great, great thing heaven is going to be", the blessing of being with his sweetheart, Lulu, and his family, and how thankful he was to be relatively free from pain and discomfort. In our frequent phone calls I tried to reinforce his focus on God and Heaven. I would read him encouraging scriptures and pray with him and for him. Those were rare and treasured times of closeness for dad and me. Together we experienced God's presence and peace in way we had never shared before. God was preparing us for what lay just ahead.

On Monday, May 3, my brother, Bill, called to tell me dad wasn't doing well. I knew dad had been having some difficulty breathing for the last few nights. His doctors were monitoring his condition and doing what they could to keep him comfortable. I asked Bill if he could call me again as soon as he arrived at dad's apartment, and let me speak with dad. Bill called back at about three that afternoon and handed the phone to dad, who was lying in bed. In labored low tones, but with a surprising sense of certainty, dad said, "It's time for me to go and be with the Lord, I'm ready to go, and I'm starting to suffer".

Startled, because dad had never spoken like this to me before, I answered, "Dad, God's arms are wide open to you now, let's pray. Lord, Jesus, dad's beginning to suffer and he's ready to come to you.

Please be merciful, Lord, and take him home to be with you". I think I prayed another short prayer with dad, asking for God's peace to surround him and mom. Through my tears, I told him how much I loved him, he said he loved me very much, and then handed the phone to mom.

Our prayers were answered the next day, May 4, at about 8 PM. Dad was lying peacefully in his bed with mom standing there beside him, holding his hand, as he drew his last breath.

CHAPTER THREE - OVERWHELMED

Two days after dad went to be with the Lord, I stood in the bright morning light at the main entrance of Comerica Park. Looming above me was the massive metallic image of dad at his mic, his mouth wide open with an exuberant call of some exciting moment in Tiger history. His open casket stood directly in front of me, flanked on each side with large sprays of flowers and familiar pictures from his life. Dave Dombrowski, Tiger GM, stood alone, dignified in dark suit and tie, warmly greeting dad's friends and fans. They were auto workers, businessmen and mothers with their kids who had lined up before sunrise to pay their respects. They wrapped single file around the corner of the stadium and all the way down the street toward Ford Field, as if they were buying tickets to a World Series game. I watched intently as they quietly and respectfully filed by, bowing their heads, tipping their caps, saying silent prayers, and even weeping. It was surreal and moving to see dad's body lying there silent and empty of his effervescent spirit, while all these people who somehow felt connected to him said goodbye. I was overwhelmed by the love and respect they expressed for my dad.

It wasn't just his friends and fans that were there at Comerica Park to say goodbye. The press was there in force. The first thing I noticed when I arrived that day was a surprising number of satellite trucks parked just outside the stadium gates. By the time I was granted access into the area around my dad's casket I saw a large group of reporters interviewing Detroit Mayor, Dave Bing. When they realized I was Ernie Harwell's son they politely asked if I'd mind talking with them. In addition to all the local Detroit radio and TV reporters and sports writers, there were writers from USA Today, The New York Times, Major League Baseball, and ESPN, as well as other newspapers around the mid-west. Almost without exception, they all made it clear they were friends and fans of my dad, not just media covering a story. Their expressions of love and respect for my dad moved me almost as much as the long line of fans. They didn't just listen and record my feelings and stories about my relationship with my dad; they wanted to tell me what he meant to them, personally. It was amazing to hear how they felt about him.

How had Ernie Harwell won the hearts of so many people of all ages and walks of life? How had a baseball announcer become one of the most popular people in the state of Michigan? Why did even the broadcasters, writers and reporters have such a personal connection with this man?

THE MAN THEY LOVED

Tiger fans all over Michigan and the Midwest had listened to his voice faithfully, Summer to Summer, year after year from one generation to the next, until he had become almost part of the family. To many he was "The Voice of Summer", the soundtrack of many of their best times and fondest memories. His voice had in someway been able to rekindle memories of cool Summer nights at the cottage up north or listening to the Tiger game with grandpa and dad on the front porch in Hamtramck.

For fifty years he had loved and cared about the people of Michigan. I've heard hundreds of people tell how he personally touched their lives. Many recall dad signing an autograph, making a special mention of them in a radio broadcast or just being warm and friendly when they saw him at the ballpark or grocery store. Others remember him driving across town to bring an autographed ball to a boy confined to a hospital bed or leading a critically ill young man into the Tiger dugout to meet the players.

He had visited and encouraged sick and hurting children, adults, and senior citizens in homes, hospitals and retirement communities. He had helped raise money for many organizations and charities that served the poor, hungry and homeless of Michigan.

He had wished thousands from Detroit, Grand Rapids, Bay City and Livonia, "Happy Birthday", "Happy 50th Anniversary", and "Get Well Soon", on his Tiger broadcasts for over forty years. He would often write notes or make phone calls to cheer up people he had never even met. Dad was tireless in doing whatever he could to help anyone who needed encouragement.

I had been with dad so many times when he stopped to talk with ushers, vendors and fans at Tiger stadium. He would ask about their wives or children by name, sign a program or baseball, and listen to their baseball stories, He was as kind and caring with a vendor or fan as he was with Al Kaline, Sparky Anderson, or Mike Illitch. He was legendary for welcoming, helping and encouraging new players, managers, umpires, reporters and even announcers. Bob Costas, Al Michaels, George Kell, Herb Carneal, Paul Carey, Joe Castiglione, Jim Price, and Dan Dickerson were some of his fellow broadcasters he helped along the way. Some of the Tigers who valued Ernie Harwell as a friend who genuinely cared about them included Al Kaline, Willie Horton, Lance Parrish, Denny McClain, Jack Morris, Frank Tanana, Alan Trammel, Travis Fryman, Todd Jones, and Johnny Damon.

There were so many players in both Leagues who considered dad their good friend it would take pages to just list all their names. A short list would include many Hall of Famers, and many names you've never heard. Dad also enjoyed visiting with the umpires in their dressing room before the game and getting to know them as individuals. He developed close relationships with many of these men in the shadows who were often criticized and ignored in baseball. I've walked with him into several umpire's dressing rooms and seen their eyes light up with affection and respect when he shook their hands and asked, "How's it going?"

What made Ernie Harwell the loving, caring, kind and gentle man that so many knew him to be? Was it good genes, great parents, or a wonderful old fashioned childhood in Atlanta, Georgia? Or was it character traits he learned as a boy, like determination, hard work, or integrity? Or maybe it was the self discipline, endurance, and respect for others he developed as a U. S. Marine in World War II. Although he often talked about being influenced by all of the people and circumstances of his life, good and bad, there was something more, something greater than his life experience that made him the man he was.

Let's turn back the clock and take a closer, longer look at my dad's life. Maybe we can discover the people, events and influences that caused him to become the man so many loved.

Perched precariously atop the counter at Doc Green's Drugstore in Washington, Georgia, slender, little Ernie Harwell was calling an imaginary Atlanta Crackers ballgame for his bemused hometown audience. His lisping, nine year old southern voice was a humorous imitation of Crackers play by play often heard on Doc's radio. Ernie's big blue eyes sparkled with delight as he called out the exploits of his favorite players. His insatiable interest in baseball, and his winsome personality made his "broadcasts" a hit with the regulars at Doc's.

Life in historic Washington, Georgia had been pleasant for the Harwells until the early twenties when the infamous boll weevil attacked the cotton crops and brought economic disaster to rural Wilkes County, and most of the South. Ernie's father, Davis Gray Harwell, and his brother, Tom, were forced to close their furniture business in Washington. Gray Harwell took his wife, Helen, and their three sons, Davis, Richard and Ernie, to Atlanta where there were more opportunities for him to support his family. Gray landed a job managing a furniture store in Atlanta, found a house for the family to rent on Piedmont Avenue and settled in with the hope of a better life in the city.

After several years of earning a better income in Atlanta, Gray developed a brain tumor. It was surgically removed at Crawford Long Hospital but resulted in him being paralyzed from his waist down. He was confined to a wheel chair and was never again able to provide for his family. From then on it fell to Helen and her three boys to pay the bills. Fortunately, she was an excellent cook. She started selling her delicious cakes, cookies and tea sandwiches to her more prosperous neighbors in Druid Hills. The boys did just about anything they could to earn money, as well as helping mom by delivering baked goods to her customers. Ernie even delivered some of her delicious baked goods to famous sportswriter, Grantland Rice, as he was passing through Atlanta on the train.

OVERCOMING TOUGH TIMES

Although times were tough, Gray Harwell always kept a positive attitude and enjoyed his life, even from his caned back wheel chair. He loved to sit in his little den in the front of the house, watch the colorful jays and cardinals flocking to his bird feeder, and listen to the Crackers games on radio. Helen was baking and filling catering orders in her small but wonderfully aromatic kitchen from early in the morning until evening, almost every day. Davis, Dick and Ernie were selling things. As Ernie put it, "things nobody wanted". Magazines, Christmas cards, and newspapers were his mainstays. In his spare time Ernie played sandlot baseball with neighborhood boys or hung around Ponce De Leon Park where the Crackers played. He had inherited his father's love for the Atlanta Crackers. Sometimes he succeeded in talking the Crackers' or the opposing team's manager into letting him be their batboy for the day. One of those days in 1930 the Crackers were playing in a spring exhibition game against the New York Yankees. Twelve year old Ernie spotted the great Babe Ruth on the field and succeeded in talking him into autographing his tennis shoe.

There were many positive influences in Ernie Harwell's boyhood in Georgia. In spite of the serious challenges the Harwells faced with Gray's paralysis, and his inability to support his family, their adversity seemed to bring out the best in them. Gray and Helen were somehow able to accept and make the most out of the life God had given them. Helen enjoyed baking and decorating her beautiful, many tiered wedding cakes and making delicious little tea sandwiches loved by her many friends and customers. Although she had grown up in a family which enjoyed relative wealth and prominence in provincial Washington, Georgia, Helen overcame her much diminished financial situation with extraordinary grace and courage. She seemed content supporting Gray and her sons with her exceptional culinary skills and long hours in her kitchen. When relatives needed temporary housing she was always gracious to welcome them. Dad told me that he remembered many relatives staying with the family during his boyhood. Ernie's dad, instead of being depressed or bitter, always had a little verse or song on his lips and a smile on his face. Davis, Dick and Ernie learned at an early age to face challenges head on with determination and a smile.

They learned the value of hard work and gained confidence that they could overcome any obstacles which stood in their way. They learned to be gracious and generous by often sharing their home with their relatives. Above all, there was a strong sense of stability and well being in the Harwell home created by Gray and Helen's devotion for each other and their love for their boys.

The Harwell's cozy Tudor cottage on Clifton Road in Druid Hills was a cheerful and lively environment for the growing Harwell boys. The small brown brick house sat up on a little rise of green grass above street level, with the towering poplars and pines of Fernbank Woods framing it from behind. The backyard was a tiny oasis of lawn and rock garden bordering the woods, where Helen enjoyed her roses, blue hydrangeas, and peonies. I have vivid and happy memories of visiting "Granny' (Helen) and "Poss" (Gray) as a young boy, with my parents and my brother, Bill. Dad would park our car several houses away, and all of us would creep stealthily through the garden and surprise Granny when she came to see who was pounding on the back door. She was short and plump and always looked clean and fresh in her long skirt and crisp white apron. Her chubby, sweet face was bright with a smile and her long auburn hair was wrapped up in a small, tight bun. She would throw her arms around us, give us a big squeeze, and lead us into her kitchen. The counters and table were usually covered with sheets of freshly baked bread or cheese biscuits, just out of the oven. Large ceramic bowls of fresh homemade chicken salad or pimento cheese sat ready to fill her little soft triangles of white and wheat bread and become her delicious tea sandwiches. As soon as we arrived in her kitchen "Granny" would serve Bill and me a warm macaroon, or oatmeal cookie, and put a little bottle of Coke in our hands. "Poss" would greet us from his big wing back chair in his den with a happy grin and some kind of a joke or rhyme he'd make up on the spot.

I don't remember "Granny" or "Poss" being irritable, angry or impatient, even when Bill and I got muddy rolling down the grassy hill in front of their house or when we got our pants soaked retrieving golf balls from the stream across the street on Druid Hills Golf Course. As their first grandchildren we were able to get away with much more than we should have. They seemed so glad to have us there that all our boyhood mischief was graciously overlooked.

Even though they suffered with Gray's paralysis and the many difficulties and limitations it brought, Gray and Helen Harwell were able to give their sons the love and support they needed. Young Ernie and his brothers knew they were loved. Their parents showed by their own lives that difficult circumstances could be overcome and that there was always enough to share with others.

My dad and his brothers, Davis and Dick, had a great start in life. Their amazing parents' love and the happy, family environment they created for their boys was a solid foundation for their future. In contrast, Gray's paralysis and the difficult financial challenges the family faced had also impacted the Harwell boys.

Dad said that the financial uncertainty he experienced growing up motivated him to make money and become financially secure. First, the destructive boll weevil had weakened the southern "cotton economy" and forced his dad to close his furniture business in Washington, Georgia, and move to Atlanta for work. Then his dad was stricken with a brain tumor and paralysis, becoming permanently unemployable. Strike three was the Great Depression.

It's easy to understand why young Ernie Harwell was ambitious. Why he would figure out a way to become sixteen year old Atlanta Correspondent for The Sporting News. Why he would convince a promoter for Tommy Dorsey and Glenn Miller to give him 10% of admissions received from the Emory students he brought to their dances at The Grady Hotel in Atlanta. Why he would work part time in the sports department at The Atlanta Constitution during high school and college. Why at the same time he would become president of SAE at Emory, the Interfraternity Council president, and the editor of the school paper, The Wheel. It's not surprising either that he became the first Sports Director at WSB as soon as he graduated from Emory.

His strong ambition and talent eventually took him to the Brooklyn Dodgers, 55 years of broadcasting Major League Baseball, induction into the Baseball Hall of Fame, The Sportswriters Hall of Fame, The Radio Hall of Fame, the Michigan Hall of Fame, the Georgia Sports Hall of Fame, and others. I rest my case. My dad was ambitious.

"ALL THINGS NEW"

When dad joined the Detroit Tigers in 1960 he'd already been broadcasting major league baseball for twelve years. In those years with the Dodgers, Giants and Orioles he'd realized some of his dreams in baseball and had also achieved financial security. During his first Spring training with the Tigers both of dad's parents passed away. Back in Atlanta for the funerals and to help settle his parents' affairs, dad was reminded how fortunate he'd been to have parents who'd given him so much love and support. It was the beginning of a new chapter in his life. He and his family were starting a new life in Detroit with the Tigers and his beloved parents were suddenly gone.

1960 was an uneventful year for the Tigers except for two crazy trades with Cleveland. Just before the season Detroit traded their batting champion, Harvey Kuenn, for Rocky Colavito, who led the AL with 42 homers in '59. Then about half way through the season the Tigers traded their manager, Jimmy Dykes, to Cleveland for their manager, Joe Gordon. Detroit finished that year with a 71-83 record, 26 games behind the Yankees.

Dad went to Spring training in Lakeland alone in 1961, for the first time in his life. Bill and I had enrolled in school in Grosse Pointe in the Fall of '60 and dad and mom thought it would be better for us to stay in Michigan that Spring.

Easter Sunday, 1961, was the day everything changed for dad. He heard that Billy Graham was holding an Easter service in Bartow, Florida, just a few miles south of Lakeland. As dad told us in his final video,

> Something told me to go over there. I went to the service and when Dr. Graham issued the invitation I went down the aisle and surrendered my life completely to Jesus. It did change my life. I'm still a sinner, but now I'm a saved sinner. God told me that my problems would still be there but He'd always be with me and that I'd have that peace that passes all understanding and I could really be a factor in bringing people to Jesus.[14]

When dad was growing up in Atlanta he and his brothers would go with their mother to the Methodist church. He said that "they sort of thought that if they stayed out of folk's way and didn't do anything real bad, they'd make Heaven. I don't think we actually realized that we had to have complete surrender."[15]

Dad was like so many of us, especially those of us who went to church as children. We grew up knowing and believing that Jesus lived about two thousand years ago in Israel, that he died on a Roman cross for the sin of mankind, was buried, and rose from his tomb three days later. Like dad, we somehow assumed that if our behavior is "decent", or as dad put it, "we stay out of folk's way and don't do anything real bad", we'll end up with God in Heaven. Fortunately for us, this is totally wrong. If our eternal destiny depended on our behavior how would we ever know if we were good enough? Would 'good enough' simply mean that the way I lived my life was 'better' or more 'righteous' than the other people I know? What if the people I knew, the people I was comparing my life with, were an inferior bunch, below the standard God saw as "good enough?" In short, how could I ever be sure I was 'good enough' to be accepted by God and spend eternity in Heaven with Him? Even if I did know that there was an indisputable standard etched in stone by God and I could fully understand exactly what God required, could I live up to that standard of behavior? Isn't that exactly what God did with Israel in the Old Testament when He gave Moses His laws written in stone by His own hand? But were God's people, Israel, able to fulfill God's law? NO! Were Christians in the New Testament able to do any better in satisfying God's standard by their lives, their works? NO!

The wonderful, liberating truth that God revealed to my dad that Easter Sunday in Bartow was simply that his eternal outcome depended only on faith in Jesus. It had nothing to do with dad being "good enough" to please God and be accepted by Him. Dad realized that if he believed that Jesus' blood paid the full and final price for his sin, he could be righteous in God's site with Jesus' own righteousness. "For he (God) hath made him (Jesus) to be sin for us, who knew no sin; that we might be made the righteousness of God in him" (2 Cor. 5:21 KJV).[16]

God used Billy Graham to help dad see that it was all about Jesus' blood, His righteousness and His perfect sacrifice for our sin that makes us righteous. We receive God's "unspeakable gift", Jesus, by faith and God makes us a new person in Christ.

When dad said that he and his brothers and parents hadn't "realized that we had to have complete surrender", he wasn't talking about earning their way to heaven through total devotion to God. He was expressing the need to surrender to God's way of salvation – faith, and not trying to earn our way by what we can do. "But to all who believed him and accepted him, he gave the right to become the children of God. They are reborn! This is not a physical birth resulting from human passion or plan —this rebirth comes from God" (Jn. 1:12, 13 NLT).[17] We believe and receive by faith God's gift of His Son as the payment for our sin. The moment we surrender to God's way of making us right with Him, we're born again by the Spirit of God! Jesus told the Jewish leader, Nicodemus,

> "The truth is no one can enter the kingdom of
> God without being born of water and the Spirit.
> Humans can reproduce only human life, but the
> Holy Spirit gives new life from heaven. So don't be
> surprised at my statement that you must be born
> again. Just as you can hear the wind but can't tell
> where it comes from or where it's going, so you
> can't explain how people are born of the Spirit"
> (Jn. 3:5-8 NLT).[18]

There is a second part to what dad meant when he said, "he completely surrendered his life to Jesus". He was expressing his decision to allow God to take complete control of his life and do with it as He pleased. The satisfaction and fulfillment dad had sought through his success and accomplishments had eluded him. He told us he'd thought that writing for the Sporting News and the Atlanta Constitution would cause people to admire and respect him. Instead, he said, the next day his newspaper columns were lining the trash can and it didn't make any difference. Then he thought that if he broadcast major league baseball and other major sporting events people would look up to him.

By 1961, after thirteen years of doing play by play for the Dodgers, Giants, Orioles and Tigers, dad realized that all of his successes in journalism and broadcasting, even the sports stars he interviewed and all those who'd become his friends, still didn't bring him satisfaction. That Easter Sunday in Bartow, he had come to the place where he knew that only God could fulfill him. He wanted God to take over. He was through pursuing fame and success, it had left him empty. He wanted God.

It was as if dad traded the life he'd always wanted, the life he thought would bring him fulfillment, for the life God had planned for him. It did mean dying to his dream and surrendering to God's dream, and whatever that might mean for him. When he yielded himself to God, as he stood there in front of Billy Graham's pulpit in simple faith, God literally made him a new man in Christ.

As dad explained later, God told him all his problems wouldn't instantly disappear but that He would be with him and give dad His peace that was beyond understanding. God also told dad that He woul use him, "as a factor in bringing others to Jesus".

> "—those who become Christians become new persons. They are not the same anymore, for the old life is gone. A new life has begun! All this newness of life is from God, who brought us back to himself through what Christ did. And God has given us the task of reconciling people to him. For God was in Christ, reconciling the world unto himself, no longer counting people's sins against them. This is the wonderful message he has given us to tell others" (2 Cor.5:17-19 NLT).[19]

Our lives are like an old house owned by us and used for only ourselves. Then God comes and makes an agreement with us to purchase our old house for His purposes. He promises to love and car for us forever. He promises to make the house what we were never ab to make it, but always dreamed it could be. What He gives us for our house is far more than our appraisal of its value, and much more than we would have ever asked.

All we have to do is trust Him, let Him have His way, and cooperate with His plans.

To our surprise, He doesn't bulldoze the house down to the ground and start over, but He totally renovates it, according to His much wiser plan.

He replaces the old outdated, barely functional kitchen with an amazingly beautiful new kitchen that is much more efficient and enjoyable. He dramatically improves the bathrooms, the bedrooms, the living areas, the closets, the garage, the whole interior of the house. It looks pretty much the same as it always looked on the outside, but on the inside it's completely new. All of the old cabinets, fixtures, doors, windows, carpeting, plumbing, electrical, etc., are gone. Everything is new.

God, the new owner, moves in and begins to use His house for the purposes He always had in His mind. What used to be a place of selfishness and sorrow becomes a house of loving and giving and joy. The old place used to be dark and depressing but now it's cheerful and flooded with light. While the old house was disorganized and dirty, now it's clean and fresh and everything's in its place.

Everything has changed. The house has been made completely new on the inside. Its new owner who now occupies it is not at all like the old man. This new owner has a new and better purpose and a completely different way of living. He does everything well and has unlimited resources and ability to maximize the value, usefulness and beauty of His house. He is bringing the property to its "highest and best use". His only motive is for His house to be an instrument of His love and blessing to everyone who enters in.

CHAPTER SIX - NEW THINGS IN THE OLD GAME

Ernie Harwell was settling into his new life in Detroit in 1961 when he suddenly became a new man. He surrendered his life to Jesus at Billy Graham's Easter service and God was now in residence. There was a lot that God wanted to do in and through dad in the days ahead. It was an even more significant new beginning than dad had just experienced in losing his parents and moving to Detroit to join the Tigers.

BASEBALL CHAPEL

One of the things God was up to with dad would later be known as Baseball Chapel. Notoriously hard-drinking, outspoken Detroit sportswriter, Waddy Spoelstra, was also a part of God's unlikely plan to reach men in baseball. Spoelstra's daughter was critically injured in a car accident and in desperation he promised God that if He spared his daughter, he would serve Him the rest of his life. God heard Waddy's cry and miraculously healed his daughter. Spoelstra kept his part of the bargain, yielding his life to Jesus and asking God how he could serve. That's where the great Yankee second baseman, Bobby Richardson, comes into the story. Bobby was a strong Christian who'd been frustrated in his attempts to share the gospel with his Yankee teammates, especially Mickey Mantle and Whitey Ford. When Bobby told Spoelstra of his failures, Waddy sensed that God was speaking. He believed that his new assignment was to organize Baseball Chapel and take the gospel to major league players. His first step was to talk with another new believer with the Tigers, Ernie Harwell. When Waddy asked dad to help him get a chapel going with the Tigers he was ready. He agreed to do whatever he could. Dad told us later in Tuned To Baseball,

> Baseball Chapel has its roots in the early informal meetings of players for the Minnesota Twins and Chicago Cubs. Led by Jim Kaat and Alan Worthington, the Twins began to meet Sunday mornings at their hotel. Meanwhile, the Cubs were doing the same thing under Randy Hundley and Don Kessinger. The teams would have doughnuts and coffee, do some praying, and listen to a speaker.

A few years later, the Tigers and other teams began to meet.

I remember those early meetings. Sometimes Waddy and I and one or two Tigers would make up the entire audience. It was often embarrassing that a speaker would take the time and effort to come all the way in from the suburbs to speak to such a small group.

In the mid-60s the group began to grow. Dave Wickersham and Don Demeter came to the Tigers and brought added strength to the group. Progress was still slow.

In 1973 Spoelstra officially organized the Baseball Chapel. The ministry spread to all clubs in the major leagues. Waddy flew to New York and laid out the plans for his program before the baseball commissioner, Bowie Kuhn.

"It was his encouragement and support that helped us get started", Waddy says.

The clubs keep on meeting on Sundays in the hotels. But it was a harried, frantic time.

"Why don't we move the meetings to the ballparks", I suggested to Waddy. "At the hotel everybody's in a hurry on Sunday. It's usually get-away day and that means eating breakfast, packing, checking out, and catching the team bus. Also, sometimes it's hard to get a room to meet in the hotel".

"Let's give it a try", Waddy agreed.

We did and it worked. The players seemed
more relaxed in their own environment. It was
easier for the speakers to get to the ballpark and
it also meant the speakers could stay and enjoy
the game. Now all the teams except one meet at
the park.[20]

God used dad to play a part in the beginnings of Baseball Chapel
and He also used Baseball Chapel to have a significant impact on dad.
The pastors and businessmen who spoke before games on Sundays
were down to earth, passionate about God, and eager for the players
to experience God for themselves. As a new man in a new relationship
with God, dad was ready to learn and grow. Those early years in
"Chapel" were just what dad needed to learn God's word and mature
in faith. The relationships that developed among the players, coaches,
and media who came together in "Chapel", added another dimension
to dad's spiritual growth. Before long dad was putting his growing
knowledge and maturity into speaking at chapel meetings himself.
Dad's love for the Lord, his close relationships with the players and his
easy, practical way of sharing his faith made him a favorite in chapels
around the league.

Dad asked me to help him with some of his "talks' he gave in
chapel. He wanted to talk to the players about Jesus as, "The Toughest
Man Who Ever Lived". I put together an outline for him and he adapted
it into his favorite chapel message. He used it with a number of teams
and with the All Stars from both leagues at the All Star Game in Toronto
in '91.

Here's the ending of his favorite message just as he gave it in
"Chapel" to the ball players.

We need that kind of spiritual strength. Many
of you are physically strong.... You have trained
your bodies to be that way over the years....
Many of you are mentally strong....You can
concentrate on the diamond; you can block out
outside interference...But how many of us are really
spiritually strong...And how do we get that way?

We get that way the way Jesus got that way--by obeying his Father (our God) and by trusting his Father...That was the secret of Jesus' spiritual toughness.

Mark 4:36 tells us of Jesus in the Garden of Gethsemane. Jesus prayed and he said: "Father, all things are possible unto thee; take away this cup from me... Nevertheless, not what I will, but what thou wilt". Jesus did not want the terrible agonizing death we knew he must face—yet, he was willing to obey his Father and accept his Father's will.

He obeyed.

Remember the story of Helen Keller. She was a blind girl. Nobody could handle her. Nobody could teach her anything. Along came Ann Sullivan and turned life around for Helen. She taught her and helped her to develop into an outstanding writer and lecturer. That story was told in the play and the movie, The Miracle Worker. How was Ann Sullivan able to teach Helen Keller when nobody else could? First, she taught her to obey. Ann spent one whole year teaching her to obey before she began any lessons. She couldn't teach her anything until she taught her to obey.

Jesus first obeyed and then he trusted his Father. Luke 23:46 tells us that when Jesus was crucified he cried out: "Father, into thy hands I commend my spirit." He obeyed and trusted.

That's the way it is with us and God. First, we learn to obey and then he teaches us about life. And our kids are the same way. They learn to obey and then they learn to put their trust in us.

When Jesus trusted and obeyed his Father he established an intimate fellowship. This gave him the spiritual strength and toughness he needed to overcome his opposition.

We can establish that fellowship with God, the same way Jesus did. By trusting and obeying. We can do it two ways. First, through the word, our own Bible. That's what Jesus did. When he was tempted by the devil in the wilderness he repulsed him by quoting the Old Testament—"Man does not live by bread alone"... "Do not tempt the Lord, thy God".

And we can fellowship with God through prayer. Jesus prayed constantly. And he taught us to pray...

So, we must be in fellowship with God through knowing the Bible and through praying...We gain spiritual strength— the way Jesus did.

Yes, Jesus was the toughest man who ever lived...Tough physically, tough mentally, and tough spiritually...

We should try to be tough in the same way.[21]

In the early 80's Waddy Spoelstra got me involved in Baseball Chapel by inviting to speak to the Mets pitchers and catchers in spring training in Florida. That summer I was asked to speak to the Tigers, and the visiting Royals and Red Sox at Tiger Stadium. I really enjoyed being able to share the gospel in the world of baseball, the environment I'd loved since boyhood. I'd spent a lot of days with dad at the Polo Grounds, Memorial Stadium in Baltimore, and Tiger Stadium, when I was growing up. I had even worked in concessions at Michigan and Trumbull the summer I graduated from high school. I had been in the ministry since the early 70's and was enjoying having dad and mom involved in my church in the Detroit suburbs.

I thought about how much I'd love working with dad in the Tiger chapel, but never mentioned it to anyone. Before the '84 season, Sam Bender, Midwest leader for Baseball Chapel, called and asked if I'd be the Tiger Bible Study leader for the season. I was thrilled! Dad and I would be able to work together in the Bible studies before games every other Tuesday night, when the team was in town. I had missed the Tiger's incredible '68 World Championship season because I was a student at the University of Wisconsin, but I was going to be there with Dad and the Tigers in '84.

Dad gives us a glimpse into the way God worked in that amazing season.

> To supplement Baseball Chapel, my son Gray was conducting a Bible study with the Tigers once a week when the Tigers were at home. I asked Scotty McGregor, Wayne Gross and Storm Davis of the Orioles to join us.

> They came over to the weight room—just outside the Tigers' clubhouse—for our meeting on Tuesday, September 4. After a short talk, Gray called on the members of the Tigers and the Orioles for comments.

> Scotty spoke first; "I'm blessed to be here with you guys," he said. "But you Tigers seem to me to be tense. I don't think you're really enjoying yourselves. You've got a big lead. Looks like nobody's going to catch you. Last year when we won the pennant and the World Series, we had fun. I'm impressed by the type of people on your team. And I know that if you win many of you will give the glory to God and not take the credit for yourselves."

"I've got to agree with Scotty," Storm Davis added. The biggest thrill I got last year in winning the championship was the fact that we were able to let people know that our talents came from the Lord and without Him we would have been nothing."

"There are some teams", said McGregor, "that I wouldn't even want to play for. But our team had the right attitude and I think the Tigers do, too. I'd like to see you guys relax a little. Enjoy the rest of the season."

The Tigers were impressed. Ruppert Jones, Howard Johnson, and the others took those words to heart.

"I appreciate you saying that, Scotty," John Grub told the Baltimore pitcher. "I've wanted to speak up but sometimes it's hard for me. I needed that encouragement."

"You've got to remember", McGregor added, "that baseball is not the most important part of our lives". It's what we do for God. We are what we are because of Him."

"I found that out this season in the minors", said Ruppert Jones. "I was feeling low when I couldn't get a big league job. But I went to Evansville and had a feeling that the Lord would take care of me. And He has."

"That's important Ruppert", said McGregor. "Last year when I pitched the first game of the World Series against the Phils, I was nervous. I had a 1-0 lead, but somehow never felt right. I lost that lead and the game.

Then, I came back in the fifth game. This time, I told the Lord the game was His. I was going to relax and enjoy it. I shut'em out, 5-0, and we took the title. That's what I mean when I say you guys have got to relax."

You could tell the Tigers were touched. I looked around the room. Most of these big clunks had tears in their eyes. They had heard God's word from a fellow athlete who had been where they were headed, and had won the World Series clincher.

The tigers lost that night and the next night, too. After that they went to Toronto and swept a three game weekend series, knocking the Blue Jays out of the race. A week later in Detroit they beat Milwaukee to assure themselves of the Eastern Division title.[22]

Darrell Evans was the "old veteran" of the team, who all the younger players looked up to. I remember when Darrell, in one of our meetings, told the other players that his dad was dying and he'd like us to pray for him. We prayed for his dad and for him that day. For the rest of the season I watched Lance Parrish, Howard Johnson, Marty Castillo, Johnny Grubb, Ruppert Jones, and others encourage Darrell and lift his spirits. I believe the unity and team spirit that the Tigers had in '84 had a lot to do with the work God was doing in some of the player's lives. It was a thrill for dad and me to see them growing in their faith and really caring about and praying for each other. It seemed to us that the Lord used the strong relationships and unity He gave the players in "Chapel" to impact the whole team. This spirit was often seen on the field by the players caring more about a team victory than their own individual success. It seemed that many of the 104 games the Tigers won that season were won by the extra effort of a different player each day. It wasn't a team of stars but a team that worked together to win. Every player was playing for the team. It's no wonder the media nicknamed the '84 Tigers, "The Bless You Boys".

Dad's experience in Baseball Chapel really helped him grow in his faith. When he was a new Christian in the early '60s, it was difficult for him to speak out about his new relationship with God. Dad admitted years later that he was reluctant to talk about his faith in the first few years after he became a Christian.

OUTSPOKEN

God has a way of helping us overcome whatever stands in the way of His plans for our lives. He also has a sense of humor. Billy Graham was holding a Crusade in Tampa in 1979 and invited dad to tell an audience of 60,000 at the Tampa Stadium, plus a world wide TV audience, about his faith. It's interesting to note what dad said that night as he stood before that huge audience, overcoming his fear to speak out publicly about his faith.

> This time of the year has special meaning for me, because in the spring of 1961, on Easter Sunday at a Billy Graham service I gave my life to the Lord. Like many people in America I grew up in a good Christian church-going family. But I had never given my heart to Jesus, and I had never spoken out for Jesus. I was a closet Christian. My boyhood ambition was to be a major league baseball player. But when I played baseball I knew I could never be a player. So I became first a sports writer but found that bylines and headlines didn't give me the fulfillment that I needed.

> My next ambition was to broadcast sports on the radio, and I did that, too. But every time I reached my goal I found that those thrills were only temporary. And I kept looking for something. And I found that something in 1961 right here in Florida at the Billy Graham Easter service, when I gave my life to the Lord. And my life has changed since then.

The Lord has put my priorities in order. If I broadcast the World Series, that's fine. If I don't get the assignment, that's alright too, because He's taught me there are many, many things more important than that.

He's also taught me that I can face and overcome my problems if I depend upon Him and not myself. And he's given me a peace that I've never felt before. I've also seen changes in the lives of the major league baseball players through the Pro Athletes Outreach, and the Baseball Chapel, and other Christian organizations. Especially in the last few years many of these great athletes have dedicated their lives to Jesus Christ and stood up to tell the world about Him. And that's why I'm here tonight. I'm no longer a closet Christian. Believe me; it is ironic that a sports broadcaster speaking over the air to millions of people didn't have the boldness to tell other people about his Lord and Savior, Jesus Christ. But those things have changed in my life now. I have come out of the closet for Christ, and I'm here to praise the Lord, and to especially praise the Lord for Dr. Billy Graham and that Easter in 1961, the most important day of my life. God bless you.[23]

Dad met the challenge of speaking out boldly for Jesus that night n Tampa. God was moving him forward, preparing an ambassador nd spokesman for Him. There would be more significant God-given pportunities for dad in the years ahead.

In 1979, my wife, Sandy, and I started a new church in armington Hills, just northwest of Detroit. Dad and mom had been pending the off season in Florida for 13 years, but were thinking bout moving back to Detroit full time. They visited us at our new ome in Farmington Hills in January of '81 and to our surprise, ecided to buy a home in our neighborhood.

We were glad that they'd be so close and could be around our children, Jeremy, Anne and Josh. They started attending our church soon after they moved into their new home. Dad and mom both really enjoyed the enthusiastic worship at our church, the warmth and friendliness of the people, and even the preaching of their son. They were an encouragement and blessing to us as we dealt with the challenges of starting and building a new church. They were always generous in both their financial support and their hospitality in hosting Bible studies in their new home. I have fond memories of worshiping there with them and the people from our church on Wednesday nights. Dad and mom were always so welcoming and hospitable to any one and every one that showed up at their house. They were so patient when our worship or bible studies went overtime or one of the people did something strange. I remember one fall night when dad was eager to watch a post season baseball game and our worship leader lost all sense of time, repeating over and over the same worship chorus. It was hard not to laugh watching dad painfully but patiently endure until the song finally came to an end and the people went home.

COOPERSTOWN CHALLENGE

That first year in their new home in Michigan dad received the news that he'd been chosen to receive the Ford Frick Award for broadcasting and inducted into the Baseball Hall of Fame in Cooperstown. This was the highest honor he could receive in Baseball broadcasting. He would be only the fifth broadcaster to receive this award after Mel Allen, Red Barber, Bob Elson, and his old partner, Rus Hodges. He was the first active announcer to be chosen. Dad and our whole family were so happy that he was going to be honored by the people of baseball, whom he loved and admired. We were thrilled that he was going to receive the highest recognition possible for his life lon contribution to the game he loved.

After the initial excitement of his upcoming induction into "The Hall", dad begin to think about what he wanted to say when it came time to stand there before many of his heroes in baseball. How could he express his joy and gratitude in a natural and genuine way that clearly acknowledged God's hand in his life?

This wouldn't be like Billy Graham's Tampa Crusade where he was surrounded by Christians and enjoyed the enthusiastic support of Cliff Barrows, Billy Graham and his staff. His audience this time were his baseball heroes. They were owners and executives, managers, coaches, players, broadcasters and sports writers from the front office, the dug out, the broadcast booth and the press box. These were the men he'd lived and worked with 156 games a year, for over three decades. He wanted to thank and honor all those in baseball who had appreciated his contribution to the game he loved. Even more, he wanted to thank and honor God in the world of baseball. He knew the Hall of Famers on the platform and the baseball people in his audience weren't accustomed to hearing about faith or God in this setting. How could he most effectively express his love and gratitude both to God and baseball?

What were the most important things for him to say? Because I was both his son and his pastor, dad consulted me about what he should say and how he should say it. I knew it would be important but difficult for Dad to speak out about his faith before his peers, his heroes in baseball, and a national audience on ESPN. I also knew that giving God the credit for his success before this audience would also be a very significant step forward for him, in his relationship with God. Dad was a great public speaker, good on his feet, and always well received by his audience. I was humbled and pleased that he asked my advice. I wanted dad to use his opportunity to tell his world, the world of baseball, that it was God that had put him in The Baseball Hall of Fame. I believed that speaking out for God on the platform at Cooperstown would strengthen his faith and his voice for God in baseball.

In August of 1981 dad and mom and our whole family (all fourteen of us) made the trip to Cooperstown. It was a memorable few days for all of us. The Tigers had rooms for our whole family at the historic Otesaga. It was a grand old Victorian hotel with wide verandas overlooking picturesque Lake Otsego and the wooded hills beyond. Every evening we enjoyed wonderful dinners in the historic dining room surrounded by baseball legends Stan Musial, Ralph Kiner, Al Kaline, Charlie Gehringer, Eddie Matthews, Warren Spahn, Bob Gibson, and other Hall of Famers.

Baseball heroes, history and fans were everywhere you looked. Charlie Gerhinger and his wife were in the room next to ours. In all my years enjoying baseball with dad, I'd never experienced anything like Hall of Fame weekend in Cooperstown.

Everything that weekend led up to the induction ceremonies on Sunday when Bob Gibson, Johnny Mize, Rube Foster and dad would be honored. Dad was more nervous than he'd ever been before. As I sat in the audience with our family and watched him waiting on the platform to receive the Frick award and give his speech, I was silently praying. I prayed that dad would confidently express his faith and give God the credit for all the success he'd achieved in baseball.

I didn't have to wait long. This is how dad started his speech after the introduction by Ralph Kiner.

> Thank you, Ralph, and thank you folks for that warm Cooperstown welcome. This is an award I will certainly cherish forever.
>
> I praise the Lord here today and I know all my talent and all my ability come from Him and without Him I am nothing. And I thank Him for His great blessing.[24]

I was thrilled with the words dad had just spoken. God had certainly answered our prayers. I was so proud of dad's bold yet humble thanks for God's blessing on his life. In his natural and simple way he said it all in a few well chosen words. No one could doubt dad's heart for God after those words. No one could think that Ernie Harwell made it to the Hall of Fame under his own power. As dad closed his speech with his poem, "A Game for All America", he added one extra line. "Baseball is a tongue-tied kid from Georgia growing up to be an announcer and praising the Lord for showing him the way to Cooperstown. This is a Game for America. Still a game for America—this baseball".[25]

AMBASSADOR

Dad had gone from a tongue-tied, closet Christian to an outspoken follower of Jesus. God had overcome dad's fearfulness and replaced it with a confidence and joy in sharing the wonderful message of God's love and forgiveness.

> For God was in Christ, reconciling the world to himself, no longer counting people's sins against them. This is the wonderful message he has given us to tell others. We are Christ's ambassadors and God is using us to speak to you. We urge you as though Christ himself were here pleading with you, "Be reconciled to God! (2 Cor. 5:19, 20 NLT)[26]

God makes it clear that everyone who is reconciled to Him by faith in Christ has the privilege and responsibility of being a messenger of God's good news. The amazing thing is that God uses us in our weakness to speak for Him! If we're willing to let Him use us it's amazing what He will do. I remember when I was a new Christian and had joined the ministry with Youth for Christ in Detroit in the early seventies. My assignment was to start campus ministries in the Public High Schools of Livonia, a western suburb of Detroit. I was so nervous standing before groups of high school students to talk about Jesus that my knees would shake and my body would be soaked with perspiration. I also remember, the joy I had in watching God bring many young people to Himself, giving them His life.

This was the same joy dad experienced as he spoke for the Lord at the Billy Graham Crusade in Tampa, and when he praised God at his Hall of Fame induction. After Cooperstown, dad enjoyed many more opportunities to share his faith with a variety of audiences. One venue he especially enjoyed was called Home Plate. Frank Tanana and Tiger Chapel Leader, Jeff Totten, started Home Plate in 1987 to share the gospel with young people who loved baseball. They would invite churches and community groups to Tiger Stadium and Comerica Park to have breakfast, baseball clinics with Tiger players, and to hear Tigers and other sports celebrities talk about their relationship with God. Over 100,000 have participated in Home Plate since 1987.

Dad really enjoyed being with the Tiger players and telling young people about the Lord at many of the Home Plate events from '89 until his retirement in 2002. Dad also shared his faith on the 700 Club in an interview with Pat Robertson, and at many churches and community groups in the last thirty years of his life.

MORE THAN WORDS

Dad experienced the satisfaction of allowing God to speak through him to people of all ages and walks of life, in all kinds of settings. But when God said He had made us ambassadors for Him, it meant more than just speaking. God urges people to be reconciled to Himself with more than just our words. He wants our lives to speak even louder. When my dad passed away in May, 2010, I listened to what his friends, his fans, players, coaches, managers, umpires, executives in baseball, and the media said about him. I listened to what they were saying when he said goodbye at Tiger Stadium and Ford Field, when he appeared at the Fox with Mitch Albom, and especially when his body lay in repose at Comerica Park. What impressed me most was that the dialogue wasn't mostly about a broadcaster or a sports figure, but about a man. Yes, there were a lot of people who remembered secretly listening to dad calling Tigers' games with the radio under their pillow. To others his voice brought memories of warm Summer nights at the lake house or the exciting World Series of '68 or '84. But most of what I was hearing was not about dad as the voice of the Tigers. It was more about Ernie Harwell, the man. The common threads were his kindness, his caring, his humility, the special things he did to encourage others, whenever he could.

Laura Berman's Detroit News column for May 6, 2010 (the day dad lay in repose at Comerica Park) was titled, "Ernie's love, kindness had no boundary". "Today, people will file quietly into the stadium where the Tigers now play—Comerica Park—honoring a man who reached people through love and language ... Anyone who ever met him—from famous ballplayers to fans late at night seeking autographs—came away with a story about his kindness and caring."[27] In the same paper Bob Wojnowski's column was titled, "Kind Spirit is Harwell's Great Legacy". "He was the most- uncommon common man I ever knew, and easily one of the kindest."[28]

Mitch Albom, in his Free Press column of May 6, 2010, said, "But then Harwell was much more than an announcer. He was a voice inside of us as well as outside of us. A voice you can still hear, even though the world has silenced it. He was a man to admire, a satisfied soul, a shining example of life lived purely and honestly."[29]

The full page announcement of dad's passing that Major League Baseball placed in the May 6, 2010 edition of USA Today was titled, "His Voice Was Beyond Legendary. His Impact Went Well Beyond The Game." "More than just a fine man and a fine announcer, he was an ambassador for the game he loved. We will miss you, Ernie."[30]

Dad had become an ambassador for the game he loved but more importantly, he'd become an ambassador for the God he loved. It was Ernie Harwell's life that impacted people for God more than what he said. It was his love, kindness, caring, his joy, peace, humility and patience that touched people's lives. As I studied the words of so many that spoke of him I became aware that I was a hearing a familiar biblical description.

But when the Holy Spirit controls our lives, he will produce this kind of fruit in us: love, joy, peace, patience, kindness, goodness, faithfulness, gentleness and self-control (Gal. 5:22).[31]

The words people were using to describe my dad were almost exactly the words God uses to describe the character produced in a Christian's life by the Holy Spirit. God, the Holy Spirit, is the one who supernaturally produces the love, joy, peace, patience, kindness, goodness, faithfulness, gentleness, and self control in the lives of Christians who are yielded to Him. These wonderful characteristics people observed in my dad's life weren't something he had done or accomplished, they were God's life in him. Remember that dad had simply surrendered his life to God at a Billy Graham Crusade on Easter, 1961. He had literally received God's life in that moment of time. God's Holy Spirit had come to live in dad to produce these characteristics of God's life in and through dad. Dad didn't become perfect. He still had weaknesses and temptations and didn't do everything right.

But dad did grow in his faith and obedience over the years as he read and studied God's word, spent time with God in prayer, and obediently served the Lord.

It's great to be the son of a man who is loved by so many people. I'm very thankful for him and the many blessings I've had as one of his children. In spite of this, it bothers me that people think that my dad was a unique person, one of a kind, unlike the rest of us. It's the unstated sense that he was just destined to be better and there's no one else that is or can be like him. It's as if they believe that the man they loved was different because he was more disciplined, more determined to be a better person. Somehow it seems they think Ernie Harwell was his own achievement. This is the other side of what I've heard listening to what people said about my dad.

I want everyone to know that the wonderful qualities dad possessed, which enabled him to touch so many lives, were the qualities and attributes of God in him. Yes, he was blessed with God-given talents. He did have great parents who taught him and his brothers valuable life lessons in their early years. He was a hard worker who seemed to get all the breaks he needed. But all this didn't add up to the fulfillment, peace, and satisfaction dad longed for. As dad told many people, everything changed for him when he understood that he could be reconciled to his Heavenly Father by faith in Jesus' perfect sacrifice for his sin. That Easter in 1961 when he understood that God's love for him wasn't contingent on being "good enough", he gladly received Jesus as his Savior and Lord. But that was the just the beginning of what God wanted to do in and through Ernie Harwell.

It's important to understand that God has three essential purposes for our lives. The first and foundational purpose is for us to be born again by faith in His Son, Jesus. The second purpose God wants to accomplish in our lives is for us to become like Jesus. God's word tells us that this is a process in which the Holy Spirit (who comes to live in us when we receive Jesus) transforms us until we're like Jesus. The third major purpose of God for our lives is for us to become messengers/ambassadors of His gospel. That is, for people to discover through our lives that God loves them, and that Jesus has died for their sins to bring them back to their heavenly Father.

But whenever anyone turns to the Lord, then the veil is taken away. Now the lord is the Spirit, and wherever the Spirit of the Lord is, he gives freedom. And all of us have had that veil removed so that we can be mirrors that brightly reflect the glory of the Lord. And as the Spirit of the Lord works within us, we become more and more like him and reflect his glory even more (2 Cor. 3:16-18, NLT)[32]

These three verses help us see the progressive transformation that God wants to accomplish in our lives. "Whenever anyone turns to the Lord," is referring to our spiritual rebirth that occurs when we receive Jesus as our Savior by faith in His sacrifice for our sin. Then the Spirit of the Lord comes to live in us, allowing us to see Jesus in a new way, and as he "works within us we become more and more like him (Jesus) and reflect his glory even more".[33]

ONLY GOD

The "old house", we mentioned in chapter five, which God purchased and totally renovated, wasn't renovated by its first owner. He had given the deed and property to God and God was doing the work of renovation. The former owner hadn't the wisdom, ability or resources to accomplish the extraordinary transformation the old house needed. Ernie Harwell couldn't and didn't transform himself. Dad had a favorite illustration he used in his speeches for many years. He referred to himself as a, "turtle on a fence post". His point was that if you see a turtle on top of a fence post you can be sure he didn't get there on his own. Someone had to have picked him up and placed him there. We're turtles and it's impossible for you or me to put ourselves on the fence post or to make our selves more and more like Jesus. Only God, by His Holy Spirit working in us can make us "more and more like him and reflect his glory even more" (2 Cor. 3:18, NLT).[34] As the apostle Paul said in his letter to the Galatians, "I have been crucified with Christ. I myself no longer live, but Christ lives in me. So I live my life in this earthly body by trusting in the Son of God, who loved me and gave himself for me" (Gal. 2:20, NLT).[35] Paul told the Christians in Philippi, "God is working in you, giving you the desire to obey him and the power to do what he pleases" (Phil. 2:13, NLT).[36]

Where Ernie Harwell is concerned, people have obviously recognized that the "old house" has been renovated to an exceptional level. What most don't realize is that the former owner (Ernie Harwell) was not the one who planned and executed the amazing transformation. God, Himself, was the one responsible for the amazing new house. After my dad allowed God to have full control, the Holy Spirit began the renovation that transformed dad into something he never could have been. It was the work of God in a man who had simply handed over the keys and stood out of the way. He let God do the work only God could do. Dad's part was to trust, to cooperate with God in His work, and to obey whatever God told him to do. He didn't do his part perfectly, he just did the best he could, and God made up the difference.

If God could do that in Ernie Harwell, what could God do with your life? Have you come to the turning point that my dad reached that Easter in 1961? Are you tired of pursuing your dreams, your desires, your way? Have you really found the satisfaction and fulfillment you've been searching for? Does it still seem like something's missing? Do you long for real peace and a sense of purpose?

Do you realize how much God loves you? Do you realize that you'll never be "good enough" to merit God's love, but He loves you anyway? Do you realize He loves you because he created you for Himself and that He gave His only Son to bring you back to Him? Do you realize that He is able to change you and make you like His Son, Jesus? Do you know He wants to fulfill the desires of your heart and give you a life of purpose, joy and peace? Do you understand that He wants to make you His ambassador, His voice in your world? Do you understand that He wants those in your circle of influence to discover His love through you?

The Good News is that God loves you right now, right were you are. You can receive Him right now as your Savior. He is the perfect sacrifice for every sin you've ever committed. You haven't out sinned God's grace, no matter what you've done or haven't done. His love is greater than any sin and His forgiveness is deeper than any darkness. His healing power is stronger than any pain or hurt you may have.

Just surrender to His love. Hand over the keys to your life. Die to yourself, your dreams and desires. Receive His Son, His wonderful love, and His life. Let him fill you with His Holy Spirit and transform you into the Jesus-like person he created you to be.

> -We urge you, as though Christ himself were pleading with you, "Be reconciled to God!" For God made Christ, who never sinned, to be the offering for our sin, so that we could be made right with God through Christ (2 Cor. 5:20, NLT).[37]

PICTURES

Young Ernie sitting with great grandmother,
Helen Quinn Foreman, about 1920.

Young Ernie sitting with his father, Davis Gray Harwell,
and his brothers, Davis and Dick.

Ernie & Lula with friends the night before their wedding in 1941 (former network news anchor, Douglas Edwards on far right)

rnie and Lula beaming with expectation the night before heir wedding in 1941.

Ernie, Lula, Gray, and Bill talking with Tiger player at spring training in 1960.

Ernie and Lula playing cards with twins, Carolyn and Julie, and Bill and Gray in the late 50s.

Lula showing young Gray how to load a dishwasher in Larchmont, NY about 1951

Ernie and Lula at Tiger Stadium in early 60's

Ernie giving Lula a kiss at spring training in Lakeland

The Harwell family at Cooperstown for Ernie's Hall of Fame induction in 1981.

Ernie and Lula in front of their Farmington Hills house in 1998

Ernie and Gray at Turner Field on Ernie Harwell Day in Atlanta in 2002.

Ernie and Lula with (l-r) Josh, Anne, Elisabeth, Gray, Sandy, Karrie, Katherine, Jack, & Jeremy Harwell (photo by Bill Eisner)

Ernie and Lula in May, 2009

Ernie in Comerica radio booth with great grandchildren,
Sam, Kitty, and Jackson.

rnie and Lula in Tiger dugout with great grandson, Jackson,
ıly, 2009.

FOOTNOTES

1) My 60 years in Baseball - Tom Keegan - Page 26

2) Stories from My Life In Baseball - Ernie Harwell - Page 92

3) The Babe Signed My Shoe - Ernie Harwell - Page 213

4) Tuned To Baseball - Ernie Harwell - Page 17, 18, 19

5) Tuned To Baseball - Ernie Harwell - Page 208

6) Tuned To Baseball - Ernie Harwell - Page 208

7) Tuned To Baseball - Ernie Harwell - Page 208

8) Tuned To Baseball - Ernie Harwell - Page 211

9) Diamond Gems - Ernie Harwell - Page 87

10) Diamond Gems - Ernie Harwell - Page 88

11) The Babe Signed My Shoe - Ernie Harwell - Page 215

12) Tuned To Baseball - Ernie Harwell - Page 45-48

13) Psalm 73 - NLT - Verses 23-26, 28

14) My Journey DVD - Ernie Harwell

15) My Journey DVD - Ernie Harwell

16) 2 Corinthians 5:21 - KJV

17) John 1:12-13 - NLT

18) John 3:5-8 - NLT

19) 2 Corinthians 5:17-19 - NLT

20) Tuned To Baseball - Ernie Harwell - Page 153-155

21) The Toughest Man Who Ever Lived - Ernie Harwell

22) Tuned To Baseball - Ernie Harwell - Page 151-153

23) Billy Graham Evangelistic Association

24) Tuned To Baseball - Ernie Harwell - Page 217

25) Tuned To Baseball - Ernie Harwell - Page 221

26) 2 Corinthians 5:19-20 - NLT

27) Detroit News - Laura Berman - May 6, 2010

28) Detroit News - Bob Wojnowski - May 6, 2010

29) Detroit Free Press - Mitch Albom - May 6, 2010

30) USA Today - MLB Ad - May 6, 2010

31) Galatians 5:22 - NLT

32) 2 Corinthians 3:16-18 - NLT

33) 2 Corinthians 3:18 - NLT

34) 2 Corinthians 3:18 - NLT

35) Galatians 2:20 - NLT

36) Philippians 2:13 - NLT

37) 2 Corinthians 5:20 - NLT

Please send any comments, questions, or correspondence
to Gray Harwell at HarwellLegacy@gmail.com

Made in the USA
Coppell, TX
09 March 2023